Science Games Galore!

D1288219

# EARTH, LIFE, AND PHYSICAL SCIENCE

## Written by
Stephen J. Davis

**Editor:** Christie Weltz
**Designer/Production:** Kammy Peyton
**Art Director:** Moonhee Pak
**Project Director:** Stacey Faulkner

# Table of Contents

*Science Games Galore!* contains 10 ready-to-use games and 10 reproducible activity pages that teach and reinforce essential science concepts. The activities in this resource have been designed to cover earth, life, and physical science content. Like the classic memory match game, the objective is to find the most pairs of matching cards using visual recall. This game supports standards-based concepts that require equivalent matching.

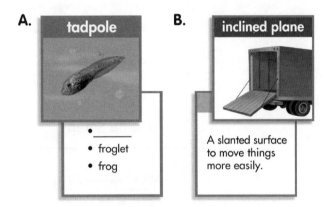

A. tadpole

B. inclined plane

A variety of reproducible pages have been provided for students to reinforce the concepts practiced in the games. Use these pages as review, as homework, or as written assessment tools. Show children's work to parents during conferences, or send their work home for parents to use in supporting their children's learning.

Students are provided practice in the following concepts:
• Plants and animals
• Natural resources
• Geology
• Simple machines
• Energy
• Science tools

The games include several features designed for both successful and meaningful independent use. Every game plays by an identical set of rules and directions. Once students learn how to play one game, they have learned how to play all 10 games. Another feature that promotes autonomy is the easy-to-use answer key card included with every game. This self-check tool allows students to compare their cards against possible matching pairs. The answer key card becomes the game's teacher. It ensures that students are learning correct information, and it eliminates the troubles that come from guessing. Lastly, the back of each game card includes a solid line to indicate the bottom edge. This facilitates game setup and helps prevent students from reading the cards upside down or sideways.

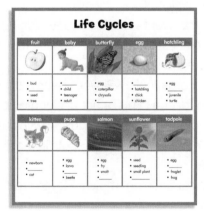

answer key

back of game card

Begin using *Science Games Galore!* today. The ready-to-use card stock game cards and answer key cards require minimal preparation. Once introduced, the materials store easily and travel anywhere students need them. Get children excited about science with the activities in this resource.

# Getting Started

## Preparing Game Materials

1. Copy card stock game cards and answer key cards if multiple copies of the same game are needed.
2. Pull out the colored card stock game cards. Separate the pieces along the perforated lines.
3. Laminate the answer key cards and the game cards for durability.
4. Attach the answer key card to a sandwich-size resealable plastic bag or small manila envelope, and place the game cards inside.
5. Store the games in a plastic or cardboard shoe box.

## Game Play:

### Number of Players: 1–3

### Objective:

1 player: Match all pairs of cards in the fewest number of turns.
2–3 players: Find the most pairs of matching cards.

### Game Directions:

1. Determine which player goes first.
2. Player 1 turns over two cards image-side up, allowing the other player(s) to see. Have students consult the answer key if they are not sure if a pair matches.
   A. If the cards match: Player 1 removes the cards and places them faceup in his or her designated pile area. This helps to avoid accidental re-inclusion with the cards still in play, and it leaves two vacant spots in the field of unmatched cards.
   B. If the cards do not match: Player 1 returns them to their facedown positions.
3. Player 2 turns over two cards, following steps A and B outlined above.
   *Note:* Students do not continue with their turn if they make a match. This assures equal playing/learning time and creates less confusion.
4. Repeat until all 10 pairs are matched. The player with the most pairs of matching cards wins.
5. The player with the fewest matching cards starts the next game. Or in the event of a tie, the player who started the game will go last in the next game.
6. When game time has ended, have players gather the cards, place them in the plastic bag or manila envelope, and return them to the storage container.

### Game Setup

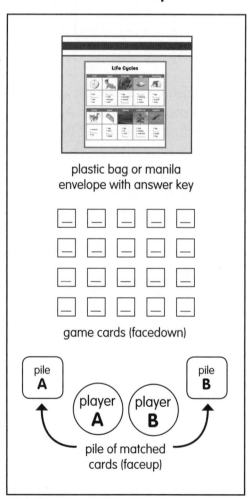

plastic bag or manila envelope with answer key

game cards (facedown)

pile A

pile B

player A

player B

pile of matched cards (faceup)

## Tips for Trouble-Free Game Play

- Choose from one of the following methods for determining who starts the first game: alphabetical order by first or last name, youngest player, or player with the closest birthday. Thereafter, have the player with the fewest matching cards start the next game.

- Teach good sportsmanship: Remind students to wait their turn, play fair, and shake hands and/or say "good game" after each game.

- Teach quiet game play: Encourage students to be respectful of others by using quiet voices.

- Teach game organization: Have students maintain a 5 x 4 game card layout, keep unmatched cards in their original positions, keep matched cards faceup, and follow cleanup procedures.

- Create a game grid mat (similar to the game cards layout shown in the diagram on page 4) on poster board or a large sheet of construction paper to facilitate the setup of the game cards.

## Additional Uses for Games

**Use the game pieces in the following ways:**

- As a transition or time-filling activity (Randomly pass out one card to each student, and have students find their matching partners to demonstrate their understanding of a concept.)

- As a method of selecting classroom partners

- To play classic card games like Go Fish and War

- As flash cards for review by individual students or small groups

- To play Around the World

**Use the complete games for the following:**

- To support the home-school connection by assigning games for homework

- To play with an older buddy class

- To make teacher-created or student-created games for themes or different skills practice using the Blank Game Template on page 16 (For example, for student-created gifts, have students make matching pictures or words about their moms for Mother's Day. Use stickers for quick game enhancement.)

- To make file folder games for individual or group review (First, separate the matching pairs of cards and glue one half of the set faceup in a 5 x 4 game card layout on the inside of a file folder. Next, laminate the remaining cards and place them inside a resealable plastic bag. Finally, have students take turns selecting a card from the bag and locating its matching card on the inside of the file folder.)

- As an indoor recess activity

- To play during a family science night event

# Life Cycles

Write the correct word that completes each life cycle.

## Word Bank

| baby | butterfly | egg | flower |
|------|-----------|-----|--------|
| fruit | kitten | larva | tadpole |

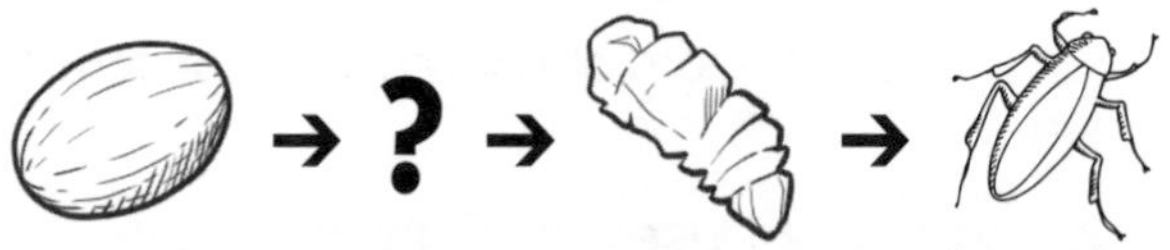

**1** bud → ? → seeds → tree

_____

**2** egg → ? → pupa → beetle

_____

**3** ? → hatchling → chick → chicken

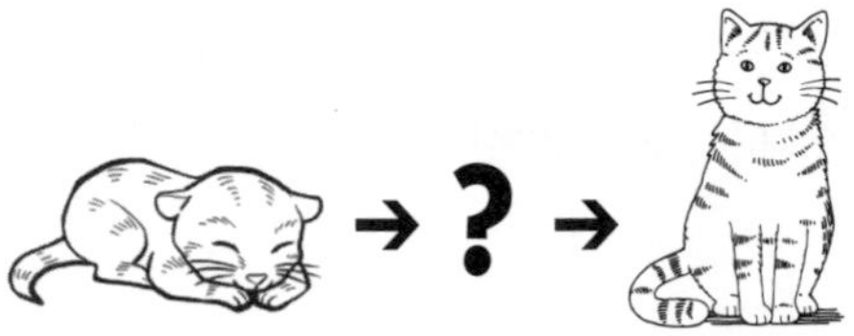

_____

**4** egg → ? → froglet → frog

_____

**5** newborn → ? → cat

_____

**6** egg → caterpillar → chrysalis → ?

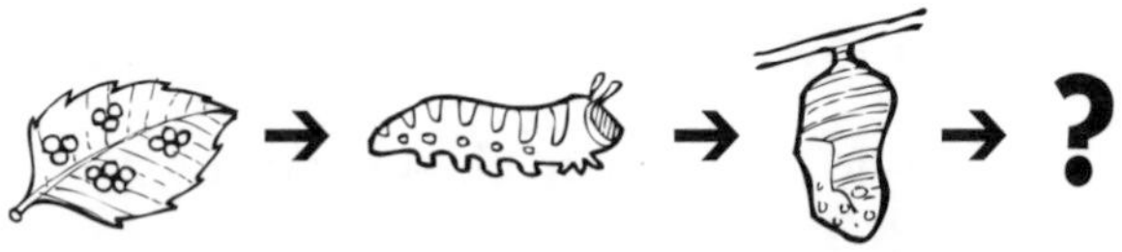

_____

**7** ? → child → teen → adult

_____

**8** seed → sprout → ?

_____

Name _____   Date _____

# Change Over Time

Write the correct word that tells how each picture will change.

 → _____

→ _____

→ _____

→ _____

 → _____

→ _____

→ _____

 → _____

Name _____   Date _____

# How Plants and Animals Survive

Write the letter on the line to match each word with its correct definition.

**1** leaves  ____

**a.** The hard covering of an animal.

**2** thorns  ____

**b.** Plant parts that use energy from the sun to make food.

**3** shell  ____

**c.** Sharp points used by plants for protection.

**4** gills  ____

**d.** A body part that allows fish to breathe in water.

**5** roots 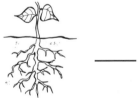 ____

**e.** The colorful part of a plant that attracts pollinators.

**6** fur  ____

**f.** Plant parts that drink up water from the soil.

**7** flower  ____

**g.** Thick hair that covers animals to keep them warm.

Science Games Galore! • Gr. 2 © 2011 Creative Teaching Press

Name _____    Date _____

# Natural Resources

Write the correct word for how each natural resource is used.

*Science Games Galore!* • Gr. 2 © 2011 Creative Teaching Press

**Word Bank**

drinking
electricity
fabric
farming
food
fuel
jewelry
lumber
roads
spice

**ACROSS**

1
oil

3
plants

5
minerals

8
water

9
trees

**DOWN**

2
wind

3
soil

4
rocks

6
plants

7
minerals

Name _____     Date _____

# Landforms

Write the correct word for each picture in the puzzle below.

## Word Bank

beach
hill
island
lake
marsh
mountain
ocean
plain
river
valley

**ACROSS**

**1**

**3**

**6**

**8**

**9**

**DOWN**

**2**

**4**

**5**

**7**

**8**

# Rocks and Soil

Draw a line to match each word with its correct description.

❶ geologist

❷ soil

❸ weathering

❹ sand

❺ plants

❻ minerals

❼ rocks

❽ earthquakes

**a.** What rocks are made of.

**b.** Water and wind wear away rocks.

**c.** The solid material that comes from the earth.

**d.** A scientist who studies rocks.

**e.** When the earth shakes, it causes rocks to rub on each other and break.

**f.** Minerals in the soil help these to grow.

**g.** This is made of small rocks and bits of dead plants and animals.

**h.** Tiny pieces of rock.

# Simple Machines
Write each word under the correct category.

## Word Bank

| | | | |
|---|---|---|---|
| ax | bike wheel | bottle opener | crane |
| flagpole | hammer | jar lid | knife |
| paint roller | ramp | screw | slide |

**❶ Inclined Plane**

a. _____

b. _____

**❷ Lever**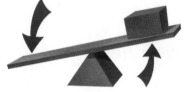

a. _____

b. _____

**❸ Pulley**

a. _____

b. _____

**❹ Screw**

a. _____

b. _____

**❺ Wedge**

a. _____

b. _____

**❻ Wheel and Axle**

a. _____

b. _____

Science Games Galore! • Gr. 2 © 2011 Creative Teaching Press

# Kinds of Energy

Write the letter on the line to match each word with its correct description.

**1** wind  ____

**2** light  ____

**3** oil 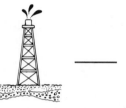 ____

**4** solar  ____

**5** coal  ____

**6** sound  ____

**7** motion  ____

**8** hydroelectricity  ____

**a.** Energy that moves in waves and helps us see.

**b.** Energy that comes from the sun's rays. Used for electricity and heat.

**c.** Fast moving air that can be used to generate electricity.

**d.** Liquid fossil fuel found underground. Used to make gasoline.

**e.** Electricity generated by moving water.

**f.** A change in position.

**g.** A solid fossil fuel found underground.

**h.** Vibrating atoms moving through matter in waves.

# Sound

Use the words in the word bank to complete the word search.

| t | s | r | h | o | p | e | g | e | g |
|---|---|---|---|---|---|---|---|---|---|
| o | a | s | o | d | h | m | d | p | e |
| a | u | o | j | h | c | c | g | l | m |
| d | r | l | s | o | t | n | e | u | u |
| h | d | i | u | q | i | l | u | c | l |
| g | t | d | m | k | p | e | s | k | o |
| s | n | o | i | t | a | r | b | i | v |
| e | a | r | d | r | u | m | k | n | f |
| s | t | r | o | k | i | n | g | g | f |
| s | a | g | r | s | b | o | h | g | p |

## Word Bank

| eardrum | echo |
|---------|------|
| gas | liquid |
| pitch | plucking |
| solid | striking |
| stroking | vibrations |
| volume | |

Draw a line to match the words to their descriptions.

❶ echo

❷ eardrum

❸ pitch

❹ volume

❺ solid, liquid, gas

❻ vibrations

• This creates sound.

• How high or low a sound is.

• Bouncing sound can create this.

• Sound can travel through these types of matter.

• Sounds make this body part vibrate, which helps us hear.

• How loud or soft a sound is.

Science Games Galore! • Gr. 2 © 2011 Creative Teaching Press

Name _____     Date _____

# Science Tools

Write the name for each tool or how it is used.

| **Tool** | **Name** | **How It Is Used/ What It Measures** |
| --- | --- | --- |
| ❶  | thermometer | _____ |
| ❷  | balance | _____ |
| ❸  | _____ | measures length and width |
| ❹  | rain gauge | _____ |
| ❺  | _____ | look at very small objects |
| ❻ | anemometer | _____ |
| ❼ | _____ | look at faraway objects |

# Life Cycles

| fruit | baby | butterfly | egg | hatchling |
|---|---|---|---|---|
| • bud<br>• _____<br>• seed<br>• tree | • _____<br>• child<br>• teenager<br>• adult | • egg<br>• caterpillar<br>• chrysalis<br>• _____ | • _____<br>• hatchling<br>• chick<br>• chicken | • egg<br>• _____<br>• juvenile<br>• turtle |

| kitten | pupa | salmon | sunflower | tadpole |
|---|---|---|---|---|
| • newborn<br>• _____<br>• cat | • egg<br>• larva<br>• _____<br>• beetle | • egg<br>• fry<br>• smolt<br>• _____ | • seed<br>• seedling<br>• small plant<br>• _____ | • egg<br>• _____<br>• froglet<br>• frog |

## fruit

- bud
- _____
- seed
- tree

## baby

- _____
- child
- teenager
- adult

## butterfly

- egg
- caterpillar
- chrysalis
- _____

## egg

- _____
- hatchling
- chick
- chicken

Science Games Galore! • Gr. 2 © 2011 Creative Teaching Press

## hatchling

- egg
- _____
- juvenile
- turtle

## kitten

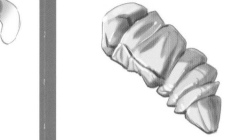

- newborn
- _____
- cat

## pupa

- egg
- larva
- _____
- beetle

## salmon

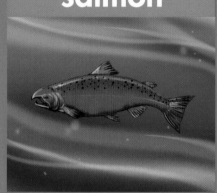

- egg
- fry
- smolt
- _____

## sunflower

- seed
- seedling
- small plant
- _____

## tadpole

- egg
- _____
- froglet
- frog

# Change Over Time

CTP © 2011

CTP © 2011

CTP © 2011

CTP © 2011

CTP © 2011

CTP © 2011

CTP © 2011

CTP © 2011

CTP © 2011

CTP © 2011

CTP © 2011

CTP © 2011

# How Plants and Animals Survive

| bark | flower | leaves | roots | thorns |
|------|--------|--------|-------|--------|
| The hard outside layer of a tree. | The colorful part of a plant that attracts pollinators. | Plant parts that use energy from the sun to make food. | Plant parts that drink up water from the soil. | Sharp points used by plants for protection. |

| camouflage | fur | gills | hibernation | shell |
|-----------|-----|-------|-------------|-------|
| A natural disguise that animals and plants use to blend in with their environment. | Thick hair that covers an animal to keep it warm. | A body part that allows fish to breathe in water. | An animal's long sleep during the winter. | The hard covering of an animal. |

## bark

The hard outside layer of a tree.

## flower

The colorful part of a plant that attracts pollinators.

## leaves

Plant parts that use energy from the sun to make food.

## roots

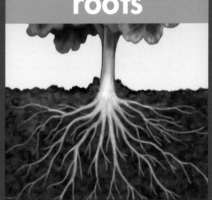

Plant parts that drink up water from the soil.

| **thorns** | **camouflage** | **fur** |
|---|---|---|
|  |  |  |
| Sharp points used by plants for protection. | A natural disguise that animals and plants use to blend in with their environment. | Thick hair that covers an animal to keep it warm. |
| **gills** | **hibernation** | **shell** |
|  |  |  |
| A body part that allows fish to breathe in water. | An animal's long sleep during the winter. | The hard covering of an animal. |

Science Games Galore! • Gr. 2 © 2011 Creative Teaching Press

# Natural Resources

## cotton

## fabric

## gold

## oil

## rocks

## jewelry

## fuel

## roads

## salt

## soil

## trees

## spice

## farming

## lumber

## vegetables

## water

## wind

## food

## drinking and watering

## electricity

CTP © 2011

CTP © 2011

CTP © 2011

CTP © 2011

CTP © 2011

CTP © 2011

CTP © 2011

CTP © 2011

CTP © 2011

CTP © 2011

CTP © 2011

CTP © 2011

# Landforms

| beach | hill | island | lake | marsh |
|---|---|---|---|---|
| • made of sand or pebbles<br>• on the edge of an ocean or lake | • mound of dirt and rock<br>• lower than a mountain | • area of land<br>• surrounded by water on all sides | • large body of water<br>• surrounded by land on all sides | • low area of land near water<br>• wet and soft ground |

| mountain | ocean | plain | river | valley |
|---|---|---|---|---|
| • made of dirt and rock<br>• higher than a hill | • body of salt water<br>• covers most of the earth | • large area of flat land<br>• often used for farming | • body of fresh water<br>• flows in a long line | • low area of land<br>• bordered by hills or mountains |

## beach

- made of sand or pebbles
- on the edge of an ocean or lake

## hill

- mound of dirt and rock
- lower than a mountain

## island

- area of land
- surrounded by water on all sides

## lake

- large body of water
- surrounded by land on all sides

## marsh

- low area of land near water
- wet and soft ground

## mountain

- made of dirt and rock
- higher than a hill

## ocean

- body of salt water
- covers most of the earth

## plain

- large area of flat land
- often used for farming

## river

- body of fresh water
- flows in a long line

## valley

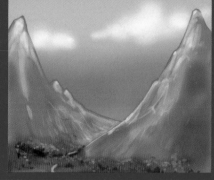

- low area of land
- bordered by hills or mountains

# Rocks and Soil

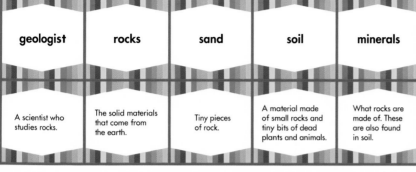

| geologist | rocks | sand | soil | minerals |
|---|---|---|---|---|
| A scientist who studies rocks. | The solid materials that come from the earth. | Tiny pieces of rock. | A material made of small rocks and tiny bits of dead plants and animals. | What rocks are made of. These are also found in soil. |

| luster | hardness | weathering | earthquakes | plants |
|---|---|---|---|---|
| How a mineral looks when light shines on it. | How hard or soft a mineral is. | Water and wind wear away rocks, making them smaller or causing them to break. | The earth shakes, causing rocks to rub on each other and break. | Living things that get minerals from the soil to help them grow. |

## geologist

A scientist who studies rocks.

## rocks

## sand

## soil

The solid materials that come from the earth.

Tiny pieces of rock.

A material made of small rocks and tiny bits of dead plants and animals.

**minerals**

**luster**

**hardness**

What rocks are made of. These are also found in soil.

How a mineral looks when light shines on it.

How hard or soft a mineral is.

**weathering**

**earthquakes**

**plants**

Water and wind wear away rocks, making them smaller or causing them to break.

The earth shakes, causing rocks to rub on each other and break.

Living things that get minerals from the soil to help them grow.

# Simple Machines

| inclined plane | lever | lever | pulley | pulley |
|---|---|---|---|---|
| ramp | seesaw | bottle opener | flagpole | clothesline |
| A slanted surface to move things more easily. | A bar or pole that rests on a point to lift, move, or hold things. | A bar or pole that rests on a point to lift, move, or hold things. | A grooved wheel with a rope to move, lift, or lower things. | A grooved wheel with a rope to move, lift, or lower things. |

| screw | screw | wedge | wedge | wheel and axle |
|---|---|---|---|---|
| jar and lid | screw | ax | doorstop | bicycle wheel |
| A winding inclined plane used to hold objects together. | A winding inclined plane used to hold objects together. | Two slanted surfaces used to cut things apart or hold them together. | Two slanted surfaces used to cut things apart or hold them together. | A rod attached to a wheel to move things. |

## inclined plane

## ramp

A slanted surface to move things more easily.

## lever

## lever

## pulley

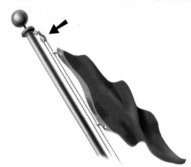

## seesaw

A bar or pole that rests on a point to lift, move, or hold things.

## bottle opener

A bar or pole that rests on a point to lift, move, or hold things.

## flagpole

A grooved wheel with a rope to move, lift, or lower things.

| **pulley** | **screw** | **screw** |
|---|---|---|
| 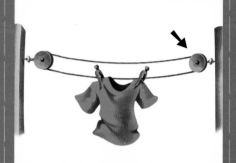 |  |  |
| **clothesline** | **jar and lid** | **screw** |
| A grooved wheel with a rope to move, lift, or lower things. | A winding inclined plane used to hold objects together. | A winding inclined plane used to hold objects together. |
| **wedge** | **wedge** | **wheel and axle** |
|  |  |  |
| **ax** | **doorstop** | **bicycle wheel** |
| Two slanted surfaces used to cut things apart or hold them together. | Two slanted surfaces used to cut things apart or hold them together. | A rod attached to a wheel to move things. |

# Kinds of Energy

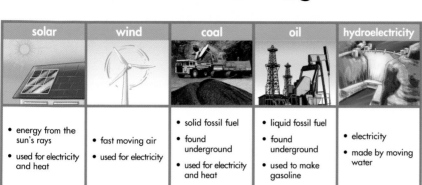

| solar | wind | coal | oil | hydroelectricity |
|---|---|---|---|---|
| • energy from the sun's rays<br>• used for electricity and heat | • fast moving air<br>• used for electricity | • solid fossil fuel<br>• found underground<br>• used for electricity and heat | • liquid fossil fuel<br>• found underground<br>• used to make gasoline | • electricity<br>• made by moving water |

| electrical | light | heat | motion | sound |
|---|---|---|---|---|
| • moving electrons<br>• create electricity | • energy that moves in waves<br>• helps us see | • moving atoms<br>• create heat<br>• used to warm things | a change in position | • vibrating atoms<br>• move through matter in waves |

## solar

- energy from the sun's rays
- used for electricity and heat

## wind

- fast moving air
- used for electricity

## coal

- solid fossil fuel
- found underground
- used for electricity and heat

## oil

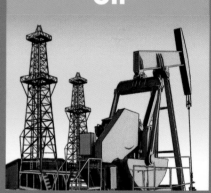

- liquid fossil fuel
- found underground
- used to make gasoline

## hydroelectricity

## electrical

## light

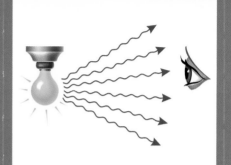

- electricity
- made by moving water

- moving electrons
- create electricity

- energy that moves in waves
- helps us see

## heat

## motion

## sound

- moving atoms
- create heat
- used to warm things

a change in position

- vibrating atoms
- move through matter in waves

# Sound

| vibrations | striking | stroking | plucking | blowing |
|---|---|---|---|---|
|  | | | | |
| These create sound. | Hitting an object can create sound. | Rubbing an object can create sound. | Plucking an object can create sound. | Moving air can create sound. |

| volume | pitch | echo | eardrum | solid, liquid, gas |
|---|---|---|---|---|
| | | | | |
| How loud or soft a sound is. | How high or low a sound is. | Bouncing sound. | Sounds make this body part vibrate, which helps us hear. | Sound can travel through these types of matter. |

## vibrations

These create sound.

## striking

Hitting an object can create sound.

## stroking

Rubbing an object can create sound.

## plucking

Plucking an object can create sound.

| **blowing** | **volume** | **pitch** |
|---|---|---|
|  |  |  |
| Moving air can create sound. | How loud or soft a sound is. | How high or low a sound is. |

| **echo** | **eardrum** | **solid, liquid, gas** |
|---|---|---|
|  |  |  |
| Bouncing sound. | Sounds make this body part vibrate, which helps us hear. | Sound can travel through these types of matter. |

# Science Tools

| anemometer | balance | clock | measuring cup | microscope |
|---|---|---|---|---|
| A tool used to measure wind speed. | A tool used to measure weight. | A tool used to measure time. | A tool used to find how much of a container something will fill. | A tool that makes very small things look larger. |

| rain gauge | ruler | telescope | thermometer | wind vane |
|---|---|---|---|---|
| A tool used to measure rainfall. | A tool used to measure length and width. | A tool that makes faraway objects look closer. | A tool used to measure temperature. | A tool used to find wind direction. |

## anemometer

A tool used to measure wind speed.

## balance

A tool used to measure weight.

## clock

A tool used to measure time.

## measuring cup

A tool used to find how much of a container something will fill.

| **microscope** | **rain gauge** | **ruler** |
|---|---|---|
| 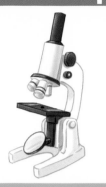 |  |  |
| A tool that makes very small things look larger. | A tool used to measure rainfall. | A tool used to measure length and width. |

| **telescope** | **thermometer** | **wind vane** |
|---|---|---|
|  |  |  |
| A tool that makes faraway objects look closer. | A tool used to measure temperature. | A tool used to find wind direction. |